ISFP: 33 Secrets From The Life of an ISFP

By Diana Jackson

Contents

ISFP: Introverted, Sensing, Feeling, Perceiving

1. Can seem socially awkward

Positive: ISFPs are true free spirits, and they often present themselves in the world with an air of total unpretentiousness. While they are totally secure in what they believe and what they do, in large groups they are less confident, but unlike more brash, caustic personalities who may use sarcasm as shield, ISFPs are endearingly awkward and innately sweet-tempered.

Negative: The thing about ISFPs is that, since they seek a liberated lifestyle with as few obligations and nailed-down responsibilities as possible, they have to rely on their people skills to get anywhere in life, and since they can come across as impossible awkward at times (especially in big, animated groups or in environments that are noisy), it can inhibit their success.

In Relationships: Being the "socially awkward nerd" is kind of cool at the moment, and with the ISFP's gift for creativity and independent thinking, they are bound to have interested parties trying to chat them up based on style alone. They might be a bit of a drag to bring around to large gatherings at times, but that's nothing a few drinks can't smooth over.

At Work: It's lucky ISFPs prefer nontraditional careers, because they might be too awkward for office culture, where falling into line is the prized trait. ISFPs aren't negotiators, they don't like situations with a lot of tension or hostility and having to face a boardroom while walking people through a PowerPoint is their idea of purgatory. Best that ISFPs work independently, away from the cubicle.

2. Has a great appreciation for art

Positive: For the ISFP, art is everywhere, not just in museums. These are the types who convince you to get up early and go for a walk in the forest with them so that you can see the sun come dappling through the leaves in the trees. In the city they'll point out a beautiful bit of architecture above your heads, something you'd never have noticed on your own. ISFPs have an illuminating way of looking at the world.

Negative: While ISFPs are appreciating art, they're unfortunately neglecting other, more concrete things, like the dishes in the sink or the bills that need to be paid. While the sensing aspect generally produces practical personalities, for ISFPs it is more prominent in the way they wish to experience pleasure, and art is pleasure for the ISFP.

In Relationships: Partners of the ISFP may feel like gods and goddesses when they see the way their mates look at them – through the eyes of one beholding a masterpiece in a museum. As mentioned, real life is art for this personality type, and that includes both the body and mind of their beloved, who is the object of their unwavering affection and adoration.

At Work: ISFPs don't just appreciate art, they love to create it, and you might find them in their studio, eyes closed, standing still and just taking in the smell of the paint or the sensation of the clay in their hands. As devoted sensualists and feeling types, ISFPs want everyone else to appreciate art as they do, and they strive to make pieces that pierce others' emotions.

3. Gifted at creating with their own two hands

Positive: Sensing types don't just want to think about it – they want to do it, they want to engage all of their senses and throw themselves into the experience. They are the types of people who can create as they go along, letting the medium tell them what it wants to do, as opposed to forcing something unnatural onto it. For this reason, what artistic ISFPs create with their own two hands is usually spectacularly beautiful.

Negative: Sometimes, when you don't chart out your path beforehand, especially in the visual arts, you can end up at a dead end creatively and find that you have wasted hours – perhaps days, weeks or even months – on a project that just cannot be brought to fruition because there was no foresight, no end goal in mind. Sensing personalities live in the here and now, but their art would benefit from more intuitive thinking.

In Relationships: When we are growing up, our mothers cherish those silly handmade crafts we bring home from school, saving them for decades. As grown-ups, ISFPs carry on that sort of tradition, but the things they make don't just have sentimental value – they could have real value on a marketplace. In any case, the ISFP's partner cherishes these handmade gifts all the same.

At Work: It is not uncommon to find that ISFPs pay the bills by selling what they make, whether it's gorgeous wooden furniture, edgy sculpture or even haute couture. Many ISFPs simply have that rare gift for creating pieces of an expert caliber, for which people will pay hundreds, perhaps even thousands to obtain.

4. Can be easily discouraged

Positive: There are a lot of stubborn personalities out there, but the ISFP isn't really one of them. These types are actually quite open to suggestion, as they are flexible in their minds, but this can work in their favor when they are pursuing a path that others – perhaps those who are more in-tune with their intuitive aspects – can see will lead to tragedy or disaster.

Negative: On the other hand, though, ISFPs can be kind of flighty, in the sense that when the going gets tough, the ISFP gets going – see ya later, alligator. As sensitive artistic types, it doesn't take a whole lot for the ISFP to feel as though their situation is hopeless, and they have a tendency to abandon ship even if the ship isn't actually sinking.

In Relationships: One of the key ways to keep hold onto an ISFP is to let them know how much they are loved and appreciated, through word or deed. As feeling types, in relationships ISFPs are always calibrating their behavior to what would best please their mate, but if they aren't getting anything back – or they feel they aren't – they'll pick up and move on.

At Work: ISFPs have a lot of great qualities that make them employable, but their tendency to get discouraged easily is not one of them. This is a personality type that needs a strong security base, whether it's a group of coworkers to commiserate with or just one friend who listens and offers practical advice for moving forward.

5. Tendency to be quiet and reserved

Positive: Imagine if the world were entirely populated by extraverts – would anyone be able to hear themselves think? ISFPs recognize the importance of being able to hear one's thoughts, especially when meeting new people, so while they might seem kind of reserved, they're actually being smart, just sitting back and observing before making any judgments.

Negative: ISFPs are actually incredibly charming and fun conversationalists, but who would know that the first time they meet? There's no law, of course, that stipulates you must be outgoing all the time, but ISFPs can let a lot of potential friendships slip through their fingers by not having the confidence to show their real selves to strangers.

In Relationships: In a way, their quiet and reservation is a veil, and the ISFP's partner gets the pleasure of pulling it back and seeing what's really underneath – which is a delightfully humorous and spontaneous personality, who has a lot of love and joy to share with the right person.

At Work: ISFPs don't normally gravitate toward big office jobs or careers that involve a lot of interfacing to begin with, but their tendency toward shyness and reservation may influence them to seek out entirely nontraditional careers, like painting or dancing. ISFPs may also take up freelancing, as graphic designers perhaps, so that social interaction with strangers is kept to a minimum.

6. Guarded, difficult to get to know

Positive: Even when the ISFP is at ease among friends, there could still be some among the group who feel that they don't know who this person really is. When faced with new strangers, however, ISFPs choose not to let people in so easily and may therefore prevent themselves from entering into hasty and ruinous friendships.

Negative: The problem with always holding people at arm's length is that you're not just holding them there – you're pushing them away. Everyone needs someone they can count on in a moment of crisis – that person who will drive you home after surgery, for instance – and ISFPs may look around and see that they never let anyone in; they are truly alone.

In Relationships: With any luck, there is someone who sees so much potential in that quiet, guarded artist that they continually seek to break down the ISFP's walls – and succeed. ISFPs are one of the few introverted types who might actually benefit from the presence of an extravert – someone who to cheerlead and make exuberant displays of affection.

At Work: ISFPs walk that fine line between being mysterious and just being a quiet drag in the workplace. The thing is, everyone is happier at work when everyone gets along, so ISFPs who find themselves with a team of coworkers should make the effort to be a little bit more open to people who are just trying to get through the day as pleasantly as possible.

7. Tendency to be disorganized or messy

Positive: Everyone has that one friend whose house is always as neat as a pin, everything in perfect order, bathrooms so clean you could eat off the toilet seat. You admire that friend, but you also hate them for making you feel guilty about the fact that you haven't dusted in a month. Well, the ISFP is here to relieve all of your guilt, because by setting one foot into their living space, you immediately discover you are not even close to be "the worst."

Negative: ISFPs might thrive on their messy, disorganized lifestyle, especially since they often feel as though they have control over the chaos, but the reality of the situation is that it catches up with them eventually. They'll miss a very important flight and not make it in time for grandma's birthday party or lose the jury summons card, forget the date entirely and end up with a bench warrant for their arrest. Not good.

In Relationships: ISFPs can be maddeningly messy when it comes to their living environment, but it is one area where they can and should make an effort if they have a partner who is more organized. In fact, if they can find a partner who is willing to gently teach them how to be more task-minded about everyday household chores, it could help the ISFP in a lot of other ways.

At Work: Coworkers who have to rely on the ISFP will always be holding their breath, right up to the very deadline, unsure of whether or not one of the essential components of the project will show – such is the ISFP reputation for disorganization. ISFPs who instead choose to work independently can spare everyone a lot of high blood pressure!

8. A very kind and gentle spirit

Positive: Unlike a lot of artistic types out there, the ISFP is among the sweetest, most friendly personalities, with a kind word for everyone. It might take people time to get to know them, but once they're in, people will wonder how they ever went so long without having this gentle spirit in their lives. ISFPs might not always make the best choices (who does?), but they do always mean well.

Negative: Kind and gentle spirits run two risks: first, they are open to manipulative and being used by others, who will take advantage of their "friend's" kindness and use it for their own sinister purpose; and second, ISTPs are like wildflowers, sweet and carefree, yet easily crushed.

In Relationships: It can be really difficult for the partner of a ISFP to say "no" to their mate, because this personality type has a way of looking at you – full of promise yet completely earnest and without guile. It's a tough combination to beat, and one that keeps the ISFP popular among potential love interests.

At Work: Finding an ISFP (who is happy) in the corporate world is like trying to find an elephant on a farm in Pennsylvania – the one just doesn't suit the other. ISFPs are prone to caring about more than just a bottom line, and the environment itself would suffocate and stifle their creativity and independence. They should steer clear, no matter what the enticements.

9. Afraid of rejection

Positive: People who fear rejection tend to tread with caution and may even have more pessimistic (or realistic) outlooks on life. In fact, that is where ISFP and INFPs most differ – ISFPs aren't as dreamy or idealistic. But that's not a bad thing. For one, it spurs ISFPs to be the very best they can be, whether it's in their personal or professional lives.

Negative: A lot of people find that when they are afraid of rejection, they opt instead to just not try. ISFPs can fall into this group. They are surprisingly sensitive, perhaps more sensitive than many of us could imagine, and criticism – or the memory of past criticism – makes them burn up with shame and embarrassment. ISFPs have to develop thicker skin.

In Relationships: Fear of rejection is what keeps many couples from ever happening, because one side is oblivious and the other is simply too scared to put themselves out there emotionally. If ISFPs find themselves in their 30s or 40s and all alone, perhaps it's time for them to start pushing outside of their comfort zone. Rejection gets easier to bear the more practice you have receiving it.

At Work: In the career arena ISFPs have no choice but to submit their work if they want to get paid, so their fear of rejection might be strong, but it can't be completely debilitating. They might find, too, that their fears are bigger than the reality, as their work tends to be exceptionally good and well-received.

10. Less energetic than average

Positive: ISFPs might not venture very far from home on a regular basis, but they have a good reason not to: they're often busy creating from the comfort of their loft or living room or wherever they have set up shop. They might not be up for a hike or a long shopping trip, but that's only because they'd rather be quietly recharging their batteries as they make something with their hands.

Negative: If you suddenly remember your ISFP friend and then realize you haven't seen them in months, that's pretty normal. Too much isolation, caused by a lack of energy or interest in going out, can cause a whole host of mood-related disorders, including depression or anxiety. ISFPs need to get outside and get some sunshine once in a while, or risk fading away.

In Relationships: ISFPs might seem sedate even among their introverted brethren, so it can be incredibly fulfilling for them to have a partner who induces them to get up and get out, whether it's a walk in the park or a dinner party with friends. ISFPs might think they're happier with someone who is more like them in terms of energy, but sometimes two wrongs don't make a right.

At Work: ISFPs definitely don't thrive in high-energy careers; they need to go at their own pace, with the flexibility to take a nap in the middle of the day if they want, or spend an hour crafting the perfect sandwich (bacon takes time to cook!). It's lucky for them that ISFPs' skills are usually geared toward low-key professions with a lot of independence anyway.

11. Does not like being the center of attention

Positive: Sometimes that diva (man or woman) who likes being the center of attention is a lot of fun, but most of the time, they wear out their welcome pretty quickly, without realizing it. The ISFP is the complete opposite, preferring to stay anonymous and going a long way toward not annoying everyone around them.

Negative: Their dislike for being the one that everyone looks at can be at odds with their gifts, which are usually so plentiful that they draw the eye and make people wonder, "Who created that?" Further, the ISFP is the type who may take their dislike to extremes and will try to get out of being sung "Happy Birthday" because they don't want everyone focusing on them.

In Relationships: ISFPs are givers in relationships, definitely the ones who will reach out and spoil their partners. They do like to get attention in return, and positive feedback will never be met with anything except gratitude and enthusiasm, but the ISFP definitely does not want their partner to make a fuss over them, publically or privately.

At Work: ISFPs are paradoxical in that they need validation for their work, but too much attention will cause them to run and hide. For them, it's always a fine line that must be walked, and it can be kind of exhausting for others to know where that line is drawn. ISFPs can do themselves and everyone else a favor by just learning to smile and take a compliment.

12. Perceptive and sensitive to others' feelings

Positive: As an introverted sensing personality, ISFPs are deeply in-tune with how others are feeling, and they in turn react with kindness and consideration. In fact, it doesn't matter if it's their mother or a stressed-out cashier on Christmas Eve, ISFPs are going to sense the emotion and do whatever they can to help alleviate it.

Negative: While they're busy caring about everyone else, ISFPs can either end up lacking time to consider their own needs or emotionally drained because they are have a tendency to internalize others' feelings. In both instances, these personality types end up frazzled and it can take a long time for them to get back to neutral.

In Relationships: Like other feeling types, ISFPs tend to be good at relationships, because they have a high emotional intelligence (and they're not afraid to use it). ISFPs might not always be in it for the long haul, but while they are with someone they are respectful, honest, loyal and very thoughtful, transforming their mates' wishes to realities.

At Work: Some ISFPs who have the discipline to get through a formal higher education can end up in social work, where their empathy and of-the-moment practicality can do wonders for people who need a little comfort right now. The artists are capable of producing the most profoundly affecting pieces out there, since the audience's anticipated emotional reaction guides them through the creative process.

13. Enjoys contributing to the well-being of others

Positive: ISFPs are nurturers who gain personal satisfaction from the ability to help other people feel good, physically and emotionally. If you're sick, your ISFP friend is going to rush over with homemade chicken noodle soup and a good book. Because they're hands-on, ISFPs like to help people in ways that can do immediate good, before their very eyes.

Negative: ISFPs can end up using their "helping others" actions as a crusade to distract themselves from their own insecurities. Since they tend to be fearful of what others think, as well as sensitive to criticism, ISFPs can use their willingness to come to the aid of others as a smoke-screen for their own fears.

In Relationships: As partners and parents, though, ISFPs are exceptionally giving and caring. Even if they themselves suffer from low self-esteem, you could not find a more convincing and enthusiastic cheerleader for a family unit. Not only do they contribute to emotional well-being, they are willing to cook healthy meals and encourage physical activity to keep bodies happy, too.

At Work: Yet another trait that helps ISFPs work well in the social services, those who can make their way through college and even graduate school will be well-poised to help many people on a personal level through therapy or counseling. You almost don't have to pay them for it, that's how much ISFPs like helping people feel good.

14. Has a strong affinity for aesthetics and beauty

Positive: ISFPs themselves tend to be put together very well, because their sensing aspect gives them an almost intuitive ability to organize objects and colors in a way that is aesthetically pleasing. And it extends to other aspects of their lives as well, such as their homes, which might not be neat, but which are decorated harmoniously.

Negative: When they are faced with something that is ugly and unharmonious, ISFPs can be at a loss. In fact, rather than try to work with it, they can instead feel offended by its presence and try to ignore it. Picture an ISFP confronted by an enormous landfill. It is grotesque, hugely grotesque, and the ISFP quakes at the sight, then needs a few days to recuperate from how horrible it was.

In Relationships: This trait does not imply, as it might seem, that ISFPs will only date hotties, because ISFPs have a talent for seeing beauty in the unconventional. It could mean, however, that ISFP mates and their families have a long life of visiting museums and natural wonders all over the country and the world.

At Work: ISFPs aren't just gifted at creating art, they make good critics as well. With their fine sense of how things should look in order to be harmonious, ISFPs could be among the most discerning and renowned art critics out there, particularly because they aren't out to hurt anyone's feelings or be mean-spirited.

15. Has an innate love of animals

Positive: Bring on the puppies! ISFPs love animals, and even if they don't work around them in a shelter or at a groomer's, they will find a way to be around them or help them as volunteers. This is also great, because if a friend is going out of town, they know exactly who to ask to dog sit for the weekend.

Negative: While ISFPs love their animal brethren, they are not always the most suitable pet owners. Pet ownership, particularly dog ownership, is a huge responsibility that requires commitment of time and resources, and frankly, ISFPs might not have either. So they could get a puppy, realize how much work it is and then break their hearts over having to return it or put it in a shelter.

In Relationships: If you're worried about your ISFP date meeting your dog or cat, don't be. They'll love them, no matter what, and animals can sense this and return that liking. You might want to nix the zoo date, though – ISFPs tend to get emotional seeing the animals caged up or behind glass.

At Work: ISFPs could very well end up in careers where they get to work around animals all day, whether it's dog walking in the city or, for the ISFPs who can stick to the rigorous schooling, becoming a veterinarian (or working in a vet's office). Further, having a furry friend at home can help the ISFP alleviate work stress, as dog and cat owners have been shown to lead happier, longer lives.

16. Loves nature

Positive: ISFPs love a beautiful painting, but if you ask them, there is nothing as gorgeous in the world as the natural world, be it the drop of dew on leaves of morning grass or the pink sunset at the end of a long summer day. They have a way of getting others to stop and appreciate the same, too.

Negative: ISFPs who get caught up in environmental activism (which is very appealing to their personalities) can get stuck in the details, and end up missing the big picture. Without a strong intuitive aspect, sensing ISFPs might only see the issues in black and white; they'll fail to understand the nuances of environmental policy change and how complex the situation really is.

In Relationships: When they can muster the energy, ISFPs love a nature walk or a trip to visit a natural wonder, like Niagara Falls or the redwoods in California. The children of ISFPs can expect family trips, not to places like Disney World, but to more low-key nature spots, and it surely wouldn't be a stretch if they prefer RV camping to hotels.

At Work: ISFPs don't really have the personality to work in and among nature (leave that to the more adventure-seeking types), but they are often inspired by the natural world, with the artistic types incorporating it into their pieces (like a furniture maker who honors the tree from which the wood was culled by carving a beautiful oak into the back of a chair).

17. Lacks self-confidence

Positive: While ISFPs might lack self-confidence at times, you can be equally sure they are among the most modest personality types out there. They are never thrusting themselves forward into the spotlight or bragging about their accomplishments; they quietly go about their business, deserving so much more recognition than they ever receive.

Negative: There are major pitfalls to lacking self-confidence, of course, namely that someone who doesn't believe in him or herself is walking a dangerous path toward depression and other mental illnesses. Friends and family can find it rather tiring to constantly bolster their ISFP with words of encouragement, and they may wonder, "When will he/she see what we see?"

In Relationships: If ISFPs are needy in relationships, it's because they just don't feel good enough for their mate, so they crave constant validation. They won't ask for it, of course; they'll internalize it, silently counting the number of days since they last received a compliment from their partner.

At Work: ISFPs can find that their lack of confidence undermines them at work in so many ways. For starters, other people can take credit for their work, and the ISFP won't put up a fight over it. Then there's the fact that they can find themselves never advancing in their careers because they're not able or willing to acknowledge how good their work is.

18. Exhibits mood swings

Positive: The ISFP wears his or her heart on their sleeve, and they wear every emotion on their expressive faces, too. Mood swings can be a touch challenging, but with the ISFP, you can tell just by looking at them how they feel (it's a nice complement for their ability to read everyone else's emotions just by being around them). This means you know to either steer clear or join the fun.

Negative: Keeping up with the ISFP mood swings can be somewhat exhausting, though, especially for those who are emotionally invested in their ISFP and care deeply for them. You never know what will set them off – a sad movie or the sight of their ex with a new partner. All you know is that one minute they were fine and the next – BAM. Uncontrollable Crying City.

In Relationships: The ISFP's partner is the one who bears the brunt of their mood swings in their adult years, so it is important that they come equipped with a solid backbone (to stand up to their mate and tell them to knock it off when the mood swings are excessive) and a great deal of patience.

At Work: It's a good thing a lot of ISFPs can make their living independent of structured office settings, because their mood swings would cause riots and drama among coworkers, to the point where they might be shown the door. Instead, as self-employed workers, ISFPs can be prone to dramatic periods of extraordinary industriousness, followed by extreme lethargy.

19. Easily distracted

Positive: There are some personality types where you could try to throw them a surprise party, but the second they catch a whiff of secretive action, the jig is up. ISFPs are definitely not that sort, and if they start to get suspicious, you can throw them off easily and effectively by bringing something else to their attention and watching them change courses like a Swiss Guard soldier pivoting.

Negative: If ISFPs have a tendency to leave projects unfinished before happily jumping to the next, it's because of their perceiving aspect, which makes them flexible and open-minded by also flighty and easily distracted. This means the ISFP can leave a trail of unfinished business in their wake, whether it's home improvement projects or their personal website.

In Relationships: ISFPs are as committed as anyone once they find the right person, but until that person comes along (and it can take a long, long while), they can get distracted from their current relationship…by the promise of a future one. They don't mean to break hearts, but an inviting smile and a new, exciting personality is just too tempting to resist…

At Work: Really buckling down and getting work done is a challenge for ISFPs. A lot of them work independently or are self-employed, which is one aspect is good for their personalities, but it also requires a great deal of discipline. ISFPs, if they want to be successful, have to learn to harness their concentration and figure out a way to manage their time properly.

20. Prefers to keep to themselves

Positive: ISFPs have a lot to offer the world, but they can only do so if they aren't exhausted or drained by constant social interaction. Actually, ISFPs can be quite social when they want to, but if they are given the choice between a raucous party and a quiet evening in, they'll take the latter without much hesitation – but they won't be just sitting around.

Negative: ISFPs run the risk to which anyone who is in isolation for too long can fall prey: depression or other mental illness. While ISTPs are, for the most part, quite happy to be alone and working, everyone reaches a point where they need someone they can really talk to, but since ISFPs can go incommunicado for so long, there might not be anyone around.

In Relationships: It might be difficult at first to get to know the ISFP, because he or she tends to be caught up in whatever they are doing or thinking about and not worrying about making chit-chat with strangers. But making your interest known to them is a pretty darn easy way to get them to come on out of their own heads and say hello.

At Work: If they do end up in a professional, have-to-dress-up-and-go-to-work type of job, the ISFP is going to be very quiet, with only a few close work friends (whose friendship took a long time to build). Those who are self-employed will wake up every morning, rejoicing in their freedom and their ability to just focus on their work, with zero interruptions from a boss or coworkers.

21. Can think independently and originally

Positive: Despite their sensing aspect, which can make more logical types err toward the side of tradition and conservativeness, the perceiving ISFP is an undeniable original, who marches to the beat of his or her own drummer with such conviction that it's enough to incite jealousy from those of us who are less confident when it comes to thinking for ourselves.

Negative: ISFPs are, unfortunately, bound to rub some people the wrong way. They aren't as outgoing or brash as their extravert counterparts, but people who march to the beat of their own drummer will always get marked out as "different" eventually, causing more traditional-minded people to view them with suspicion, distaste or outright fearful persecution.

In Relationships: ISFPs are a wonder to be involved with romantically, because they have a way of observing things that makes you think about a tree or a book in a totally new light. Their refreshingly unpretentious and unconstrained way of viewing the world is at once exciting, enticing and illuminating.

At Work: INFPs tend to get the bulk of the credit for creative ideas, but ISFPs are equally creative and innovative – they just use different mediums. It is through these mediums that ISFPs can often build a career that is successful and significant, because the independent and original way that they look at the world is reflected in their work.

22. Values their personal space

Positive: Some people don't know when to say "enough is enough," and they end up giving up more of themselves than they can comfortably handle. ISFPs do find it difficult to say "no" on occasion, but never when it comes to their personal hula hoop of space, which they guard with the ferocity of a mama bear over her cubs, thus preserving their sanity.

Negative: Just where is the line between the ISFP's personal hula hoop of space and the rest of the world? Well, that might only be clear to them, so unsuspecting people can trample over the border, not meaning any harm, and find themselves being escorted unceremoniously out again. ISFPs are difficult to get to know, and this doesn't help.

In Relationships: When we are in a relationship with someone for a long time, we start to find our lives and even our minds blending into one. There are pluses and minuses to this phenomenon, but ISFPs are keenly aware of their need for space and for personal identity, so it's unlikely they will ever fall too far down this rabbit hole.

At Work: Their need for personal breathing room is part of what prompts ISFPs to seek out self-employment, whether they're painting in a studio loft or walking dogs for the affluent in a big city. ISFPs really value the knowledge that people aren't going to come trampling all over their Zen, and this extends to their professional lives.

23. Appreciates people who support their goals

Positive: You can earn the ISFP's everlasting love and devotion by showing them a little support in the things that they want to accomplish. If they're part of a dog rescue and you show up at their fundraiser, you're golden; if they are having a gallery showing for their latest sculpture and you bring a friend to the opening, expect to have a BFF for life. You, in turn, cannot help but be charmed by their genuine appreciation.

Negative: It's not to say that if you don't support their goals you are dead to the ISFP, but there is definitely a chilly breeze coming from their direction if you were supposed to show up at one of their events and you didn't. But that's not always fair; stuff comes up, people have busy lives, but the ISFP can be kind of petty about it.

In Relationships: Sometimes the right person for us is the one who flies under the radar, who is too shy or scared to say anything, but continuously shows their feelings by just being there. ISFPs appreciate these people, but maybe one of them is the right person for a relationship – they just have to open their eyes to the possibility!

At Work: ISFPs, whether they are in an office setting as a social worker or a crochet artist who sells her crafts on Etsy, need positive feedback in order to flourish in their chosen profession. Despite how independently they are capable of thinking as part of their creative process, in the grand scheme of things, only a shining review of their work or performance will inspire them to keep chugging along.

24. Mistaken for being carefree; actually takes life very seriously

Positive: Hey, no one could blame you for looking at your ISFP friend and thinking, "What a life. No responsibilities, no worries." It might bother them sometimes, because their outward impression is one of irresponsibility, while inwardly they value both progress and success, but the ISFP doesn't mind being an underdog – it makes victory that much sweeter.

Negative: It can be a drag, though, for the ISFP when those around them who qualify as "authority figures" – bosses, parents, even friends with nine-to-fives and families – take it upon themselves to constantly harp on their free-wheelin' employee/child/friend. A little ribbing is one thing, but ISFPs can find themselves subject to a great deal of annoying nagging, which is completely unnecessary.

In Relationships: The partner of the ISFP might be shocked to discover how goals-oriented their mate actually is, because he or she puts on quite a good show of not caring. The perceiving aspect, which gives ISFPs their trademark insouciance, actually describes how people look at ISFPs, not how they really are deep down. Partners who get to see the person underneath the veil are truly privileged.

At Work: ISFPs are not terribly motivated by wealth or fame (though their skills certainly merit both), but that doesn't mean they don't value professional success – they simply measure it by different standards than your typical office drone. This can be confusing for employers (or even concerned parents). Not to worry – the ISFP knows exactly what he or she is about.

25. Action-oriented

Positive: The nice thing about ISFPs is that, unlike their more philosophical cousins the INFPs – who prefer to contemplate a decision – they take a more hands-on approach to life-living, preferring action to pondering. While they might not always be the most decisive or the most logical, at least they're willing to try new things and figure them out as they go.

Negative: Figuring things out as you go can end spectacularly or, conversely, can blow up in your face and leave you with singed eyebrows. It's admirable that ISFPs are willing to jump in feet-first, but because they are not the most logical personality type, their decision-making process can be a bit flawed.

In Relationships: As sensing types who experience the world through touch, taste, smell, hearing and sight, ISFPs are exceptionally devoted partners who attend to their mates' physical needs in ways that please the soul, like cooking decadent meals or knitting blankets that were made for snuggling.

At Work: As action-oriented employees it is not uncommon to find even this most introverted of personalities working with the public and actually enjoying themselves. Through action, even if it does require much face-to-face interaction, ISFPs can see their goodwill put to use for the people who need it most.

26. Rarely uses logic to make decisions

Positive: Like other feelers, the ISFP considers how an action would make them and others feel, rather than whether or not it makes sense or is reasonable. While this course of action would be anathema to thinkers, it makes feelers much more popular and well-liked, which in turn enables them to accomplish more (it's all about who you know).

Negative: Life is all about balance, and for ISFPs, the balance is tipped toward the emotional when it comes to making choices. Unfortunately, this can turn out badly, much more often than it does for people who think and act based on sound rationale, and while ISFPs are good at rolling with the punches, taking a hit yet moving forward, bad, emotionally-based decisions can leave lingering consequences.

In Relationships: If ISFPs are with thinking personalities, watch out – there is no telling how intense the arguments can get. Yet at the same time, the ISFP might benefit from being with someone whose logical approach to life teaches them steadiness and the importance of reason, while they themselves can impart emotional intelligence on their mates.

At Work: ISFPs who work in the creative/visual arts benefit from making senses-based emotional choices when it comes to their projects – art is, after all, an extension of the human heart. Even those who work in the social services can do so much good when they act based on compassion and empathy, rather than reason.

27. Thoughtful and aware of others

Positive: ISFPs are deeply concerned about their fellow humans, stranger, friend or family, and they show it in everything that they do. ISFPs might be selfish or greedy when it comes to personal space and "me-time," but every single day they try to make the world a better place by showing little acts of kindness to all.

Negative: ISFPs can become humble-brag martyrs if they aren't careful, the types of people who complain, "If only I could have more time to paint, except that I am so busy helping the poor!" They do sincerely care, but their words can sound just the opposite – more like they are doing good to keep up with appearances.

In Relationships: The partners and families of ISFPs often find themselves utterly spoiled, their every whim catered to before they even realize they wanted something. ISFPs have to ensure that they aren't creating monsters in the wake of their constant thoughtfulness, while ISFPs' mates and partners have to stop and say a heartfelt "Thank you."

At Work: Such practical thoughtfulness is the basis for many a profession, from home healthcare workers to grief and crisis counselors. ISFPs are capable not just of listening and empathizing; their sensing aspect is geared toward real-life solutions that make a difference, starting on day one.

28. Seeks meaning in people and things

Positive: The things that happen to us in life are unexpected, sometimes unfair, but always experiences from which we can learn about ourselves and the world. ISFPs don't care to go through life believing that everything is random; even the worst situation must have some meaning to this personality type, who is more optimistic than they might allow.

Negative: What is unfortunate is that those terrible situations – a death, a tragic job loss, etc. – can be analyzed backwards and forwards and yet not make sense. And sometimes, people act completely out of spite, without any logical reason for doing so. ISFPs can end up wasting a lot of their own lives trying to find meaning where there truly is none.

In Relationships: Even the messiest break-up for the ISFP isn't the end of the world for this personality type. They are surprisingly resilient, despite their penchant for overwrought emotion, usually because they can take a step back and appreciate what their ex brought to their life and what they learned.

At Work: One of the reasons ISFPs make such good artists is because they can find meaning in people and objects, meaning that might not be noticeable to others (and so is very exciting for the art world). While intuitives tend to be more apt in this area, artistic ISFPs will nonetheless have a well-developed intuitive aspect which is just overshadowed by their sensing function.

29. Is very warm and sympathetic

Positive: If someone in their life needs to hear that their ex is a piece of trash, the ISFP is there to provide that vindication. As sympathetic sorts, they are fiercely loyal to their friends and family and will do or say whatever it takes to make them feel better about the wrongs in their life.

Negative: Does that mean that ISFPs will sometimes say what they have to, even if they don't necessarily believe in it? Of course, but we all do that to some extent. Still, it's one of the few insincere aspects to the ISFP, who is only doing it to bring comfort to others.

In Relationships: There is nothing like coming home to an ISFP after a long, difficult day, because if you were giving them advanced warning, they'll likely have your favorite drink ready and will be more than happy to treat you to a little shoulder rub. Ahhh, bliss.

At Work: Coworkers have a shoulder to cry on or an ear to bend when the boss goes after them for some error, and even the boss might open up to the ultra-sympathetic ISFP, who will no doubt sit there uncomfortably, wishing they could be anywhere else.

30. Can seem overly carefree

Positive: ISFPs definitely have what everyone would call "a lifestyle," whether they willed it into being by sheer force of personality or because they were born into a wealthy family that gave them tons of freedom (not unheard of). The way they float through life, seemingly without a care, is both infectious and inspiration, reminding us all not to take anything too seriously.

Negative: Because they appear to be so utterly without responsibility, others can come down hard on ISFPs, calling them immature or lazy. This can be incredibly hurtful to this personality type, not just because they are incredibly sensitive; ISFPs thrive under a stream of praise, and flounder in their endeavors, both personal and professional, when criticized.

In Relationships: ISFPs have to be careful because, like many people who live a carefree existence, when the time comes that they want a spouse and children, it could be that no one will take them seriously enough, or they don't know where to start in getting that kind of life.

At Work: Another area where ISFPs have find that they have a difficult time being taken seriously is in the career arena, where even the artists might be written off as too irresponsible. What they have to do is prove everyone wrong by asserting their firm practical side and getting stuff done.

31. Shows their feelings through actions, not words

Positive: INFPs are the writers, while ISFPs, with their sensing function firmly engaged, are the doers and the makers. When they are sad, they might draw the most exquisitely yearning self-portrait; when they are happy, they'll have a rare moment of abandon and drag a friend to a jazz club for dancing and drinks. The gestures that the ISFP makes to show their feelings express far more than words ever could, and they light up the world with beauty.

Negative: Actions, however, are often more open to interpretation than words. Whereas telling someone, "I just don't think that dress is right on you," is direct and cannot be misconstrued, a noncommittal shrug might seem to be enough of a deterrent from the ISFP's perspective, but is not for the unfortunate friend who ends up buying the ill-fitting garment.

In Relationships: ISFPs can have issues with people not knowing that they aren't interested any longer, because again, their actions can send mixed signals. Telling someone, "I'm not interested in seeing you again," is very different from accepting their kiss but making a horrible face that cannot be seen, because the kisser has his or her eyes closed.

At Work: If the ISFP is having a bad day at work, watch out. There will be no advanced warning for Hurricane ISFP, which can tear through in a storm of passive-aggressive door slamming and "harrumphing." Don't try to coax "what ails ya" out of them...just let the tempest past and they'll be right as a rivet in no time.

32. Not a natural leader

Positive: Not everyone can be a leader, and indeed, the world does not need a whole crowd of them. It is right and natural that ISFPs do not seek to take control of others to care to boss people around. ISFPs are just busy doing what they do, and they are too busy to care or worry about what others think.

Negative: Unfortunately, there are moments in the ISFP's life where the ability to take control of the situation and the people present would serve them well, especially in times of crisis. Yet the ISFP will freeze up or look for anyone – *anyone* – else to handle the problem. ISFPs sell themselves too short when it comes to leadership, because while they might not like it, they could be great at it.

In Relationships: The age-old couples argument of "where should we eat?" is not going to be solved by the ISFP, whose response is, invariably, "I don't care. Wherever you want to go." ISFPs like when their mates, male or female, take the lead and make the decisions. But it's not to imply that they'll always follow.

At Work: ISFPs would rather avoid leadership positions, such as manager or "head" whatever, because their innate impulse is to keep their responsibilities at a minimum, allowing them the greatest possible freedom. This is why ISFPs like freelance work or self-employment – they are leader and follower all at once and no one relies on them, nor do they have to rely on anyone else.

33. Self-critical

Positive: It's good to be able to view oneself from a place of critique, because no one is perfect and we can all improve. ISFPs view themselves as evolving works-in-progress, and it's wholly endearing to see an ISFP earnestly working toward self-improvement.

Negative: The problem is that ISFPs come down really hard on themselves, perhaps harder than any other personality type. There are perfectionists, and then there are ISFPs, who are capable of getting too much inside their own heads with the negative critiques.

In Relationships: Partners of the ISFPs may find that they have a lot of damage to undo, damage that has been self-inflicted over the course of years, all of which has led to low stores of confidence. If the ISFP is lucky, he or she will find someone patient and generous with their affections to overcome a lifetime of negative self-image.

At Work: Where self-critique is most balanced in the ISFP's life is their career, because while they might be especially harsh on themselves (e.g. berated themselves over and over for the awkward thing they said to the stranger in line at the café), they do have the sense to see that what they create is of superior quality. Artists especially benefit from the self-critical mindset, as it drives them to produce work that gets better and better.

www.ingramcontent.com/pod-product-compliance
Lightning Source LLC
Chambersburg PA
CBHW070507290526
45790CB00003B/1132